[LIGHT IN ARCHITECTURE]

BETA-PLUS

[LIGHT IN ARCHITECTURE]

A project by Guillaume
Da Silva. Modular
Nomad ceiling fittings.

4-5
The office of architect Lie Ulenaers.
The workplace is lit by Nomad
Modular fittings. Built-on spotlights of
Kreon (Regard Double) left and right
of the table.

[CONTENTS]

8-9
A project by interior architect
Guillaume Da Silva.
The big black lampshades above the
kitchen have been custom made.
At the left of the picture a sculpture
made by Catalano.

[FOREWORD]

A whole new look at architectural lighting, both for the interior and exterior.
An inspiring photographic book with hundreds of creative applications in private homes and gardens.

Wim Pauwels
Publisher

A project by iXtra, the interior bureau of Filip Vanryckeghem. Integrated Kreon Down in-Line 76 spotlights were chosen for above the bath (covered by glass - as in the IP44-standard – for the shower cubicle on the foreground).

12-13
The integrated basic lights in the wall and ceiling were combined with specific Kreon built-on fittings (light fitting Kreon / Prologe 80 on-Regule) in this project by iXtra (Filip Vanryckeghem).

PART I

$$\big[\text{ LIGHT IN AND AROUND THE HOUSE } \big]$$

ENTRANCE HALLS

Indirect LED lights of Kreon
provide a special atmosphere in
this entrance hall designed by
architect John Pawson.

Seven different applications with Kreon lights:
Left-hand page top left: Totem Floor (interior architecture: M ar S Architects).
Alongside: Dolma 145 (Kree interior, architect Frederic Leers).
Bottom of this page: the Prologe 80 Ligna in-Line, a continuous light line with innovative OLDP optics (project: Glenn Sestig for De Puydt Haarden).

On the right-hand page: top left Small Square Side (project The Heating Company), top right the Mini Side in-Line with mat reflectors (project Themenos). Bottom left Aplis in a project by Serge Roose & Partners, Bottom right Down in-Line 76 (job by Atelier 229, Marc Haenen architects).

Flush Dynamix of Modular:
A project by Van Oosterom Pilotstores in Rotterdam.

The Horizon 124 wall fittings of Deltal ght are
made of aluminium and are in the colcur white.

Vectus 40 of Wever & Ducré.

Architectural light in all its dimensions by Wever & Ducré:
models Box, Impact and Lito.

PVD Verlichting was founded 25 years ago by Patrik van Daele.
PVD is also the designer and distributor of White Line (see photos on this page) as well as the distributor of several top ranges (e.g. Kreon, Secto Design).
Bottom photo: an interior design by interior decorator Marc Guinee.

The "Brick in the Wall" concept stands for the seamless integration of light: a minimalistic design driven by functionality, with light and architecture as a real amalgam.

Brick in the Wall developed Calcyt, a heat-resistant plaster-chalk with a high density and extreme hardness. These chalk "fittings" can be easily painted in the same colour as the wall or ceiling.

SITTING ROOMS

Dimmable Cadre 1500
light fittings by Kreon.
covered in black leather.
A project by Glenn Sestig
for De Puydt Haarden.

Ceiling spotlights Aplis, a round recessed light appliance of Kreon, chosen by architect Glenn Sestig for De Puydt Haarden.

Four Kreon-applications:
Top left Regard semi built-in spotlights in the ceiling.
Top right Kwadro Recessed in the Poliform showroom of Miami. Four different light sources can be directed independently.
Bottom left Down in-Line 155 in a project by Peter Ivens and Kurt Bruggeman.
Bottom right a project for Wals' Wonen (interior architect Ben Van Duin) with Prologe 145 on-Regule current rail system.

These living rooms are also lit by Kreon fittings:
Top left Regard lights in a project by PCP Architects.
Top right Regard Double in a private house in Paris designed by Laure Marty Perin.
Bottom left and right Square Side and Mini Side, both in a private house in Miami.
Bottom right Diapason in a project by Atelier 229, Marc Haenen architects.

Two completely different light atmospheres by Modular: top the Nomad 4x AR111 in a project by Restyling Buro Marnix Verstraeten in Ostend, bottom the Multiple Trimless 1x AR111.

The light fittings in this house in Delft are Modular (LC Max CDM-R PAR30).

Three more examples of architectural lights, drawn by Wever & Ducré: models Solid, Rilox and Eos (4x50W Square).

Target 2 built-on spotlights by Deltalight.

The "invisible" lights of Brick in the Wall: an ingenious concept based on the heat-resistant, extremely durable Calcyt plaster chalk.

The PH Snowball hanging lamp, designed by Poul Henningsen and made by Louis Poulsen, is a real design classic. Distributed in the Belux by Hugo Neumann NV.

DINING ROOMS

Nomad minimum E27 tall
(Modular Lighting
Instruments) in a project
by A.R.T. studio.

Nomad 4x AR111 ceiling spotlights are combined with Izar LED Moodswing in this project by Restyling Buro Marnix Verstraeten.

Three times Down in-Line fittings by Krəon in a project by Kasba.

Cadre, Regard Double and Down in-Line 76 fittings of Kreon were combined in this apartment, designed by Laure Marty Perin.

Mini Side in-Line wall lights.

A project by architect Jan Elewaut. An Onn-Air fitting of Kreon above the table. The specific reflector develops a broad radiation light pattern. An ideal solution where a soft, non-glare light is needed.

Quadra Mono and duo of Wever & Ducré: integrated wall spotlights in silver and black.

KITCHENS

Prologe 145 built-on spotlights of Kreon in a project by Minus.

Down in-Line 76 fittings of Kreon. A project by architect Jan Elewaut.

Erubo on-Track profile system of Kreon in a project by PCP Architects.

Prologe 80 of Kreon generates light within discrete, simple architectural volumes. A project by Peter Ivens and Kurt Bruggeman.

Top photo:
recessed spotlights
Deep MR16 of
Wever & Ducré;
bottom a Snap-3
light fitting above
the kitchen bar.

Grid In recessed spotlights of Deltalight provide a cosy atmosphere in this living kitchen.

Quad 12V built-on fittings of Deltalight.

BATHROOMS
AND BEDROOMS

A wall spotlight Halosun of Deltalight and indirect lights under the bath, also of Deltalight.

Carree GT-recessed spotlights of Deltalight were combir ed with Kosmo wall lamps of the same make in this bathroom.

The Minigrid On fittings of Deltalight are available in black and white.

Peter Ivens and Kurt Bruggeman chose Kreon Down in-Line 153 fittings for this house on the coast.

A special reflector measurement of Onn-Wall (Kreon), an ideal light appliance for the illumination of decorative ceilings. A job by PCP Architects for Carbon Hotel.

Artist studio 229 (Marc Haenen Architects) here chose Small Side in-Line of Kreon.

Prologe 80 fittings of Kreon in a house furnished by Laure Marty Perin.

Four Wever & Ducré applications in the bathroom: top left Box III, bottom left Nin.
Both photos right show Snap light fittings.

Claire Bataille and Paul ibens chose the Totem Floor lighting unit for the Kreon Guest room in Antwerp.

Small Diapason of Kreon in the showroom of Poliform in Miami.

Down in-Line 76 recessed spotlights of Kreon in this project by Atelier 229 (Marc Haenen Architects).

A Hide MR16 recessed spotlight of Wever & Ducré.

B-Flex H of Deltalight: bendable ceiling spotlights and indirect lights behind the end of the bed.

Discrete atmosphere light by Brick in the Wall.

SPACES FOR WORK

Down fittings of
Kreon in a project by
Minus.

57-61
A public notary's office designed by architect John Pawson on the Belgian coast. Down in-Line 76 ceiling spotlights of Kreon, in combination with indirect lights.

Aplis of Kreon, standard fitting of a softening lens and light filter. A project by PCP Architects.

Aplis Wallwasher in the Kreon Creative Space in Brussels.

Cadre fitting of Kreon in an office furnished by Adikta (Gary Weberman).

The Kasba offices in Brussels are lit by Cadre fittings of Kreon.

Round Up fittings of Kreon in La Garnerie, the office with a feeling of home by Themenos.

Kreon Prologe 145 fittings in a Parisian private house, designed by Laure Marty Perin.

Regard Double ceiling semi built-in spotlights of Kreon.

Brick in the Wall integrated ceiling spotlights provide an intimate atmosphere in this area.

Power Qubo light fitting of Wever & Ducré above this dining table.

The offices of PVD Verlichting itself, fully equipped with White Line fittings, a creation of Patrik van Daele, founder of this company.

Jeti SW of Deltalight: light as the object.

Modular Nomad 4x AR 111 lights
were used in this project.

LIGHT IN THE GARDEN AND AROUND THE HOUSE

A private house designed by architect Bruno Albert, illuminated by Kreon recessed spotlights.

Dolma 80 Outdoor of Kreon: a recessed element, built up around an aluminium shape, which can be integrated into walls.

Cadre QR-CBC51 of Kreon in a Minus-project in Poperinge.

Mini Rokko of Kreon offers poetic light accents. A project by Paul Wijnants.

Light plays a primordial role in this renovation of a mansion in Brussels by Joël Claisse.

Two examples of one of the successful products in the outdoor
collection of Wever & Ducré: Tube Carré.

Deltalight has a wide range of outdoor light fittings.
Top left Carree X recessed spotlights, alongside PUK XL.
Bottom left Villa light columns and alongside Genie 200 floor spotlights.

Carree X recessed spotlights of Deltalight, integrated in the roof overhang.

Basic R of Deltalight provides cosy accents.

Three more applications with Deltalight: top the Genie 200 floor spotlights, bottom left Walker and bottom right Labyrinth light columns.

PVD Verlichting is a specialist in timeless, high quality garden lights Simply and Nona.

Various Modular light elements were used in this house: Boxlite halogen wall spotlights (top left), Fuser Double (top right) and Juliette Foot Ministar (bottom of this page).

The PH3 Bollard Outdoor Lamp, designed by Poul Henningsen for Louis Poulsen, was already considered a masterpiece 40 years ago.
This lamp is today mainly praised because of the downwards appearing, multi-shadow system, which is also anti-glare.
Hugo Neumann NV is the exclusive Belux importer of Louis Poulsen.

PART II

[INSPIRATIONAL PROJECTS]

[A SPECIAL METAMORPHOSIS

The commission consisted of creating a cosy atmosphere in a contemporary home with 5.5 m high south facing glass segments.

The original straight staircase was replaced by a lower pitch stair that starts in front of the window frame by means of a plinth in flamed bluestone from Hainaut.

The self-supporting steps are in stained oak, lit with LEDs.
PUK4 type lamp, varnished black, from the Deltalight collection.
The walls are covered in dark stained oak with integrated black varnished aluminium banister.

88-89
The 2.7 m long gas hearth with steel, black lacquered plinth was produced by Metalfire.
A Chantecaille reading light in black epoxy from Christian Liaigre.

The dining and living room table were made from stained oak, according to a design by the interior architect
Frederic Kielemoes.
The floor is in flamed bluestone.

Frederic Kielemoes

Interior architect

Brugstraat 53

B – 8850 Ardooie

T +32 (0)486 40 75 64

www.frederickielemoes.be

info@frederickielemoes.be

90
The incidence of light in the office space is filtered
through a curtain of horizontal wooden slats.
All the furniture in dark stained oak with
integrated T5-lighting.
Ceiling lighting of the Carree type from
Deltalight.

HARMONY
IN SAVANNAH BLUE

S avannah Blue is a special natural stone with a lot of shades.
With this floor as the base the interior architect Frederic Kielemoes created a design where all the colours were repeated in the interior design and the selection of furniture.
An office is concealed behind the curved wall, which starts from the hall.
This wall has been painted in a dark, graphite colour and ensures depth from the living area.

The low position of the wall lighting (type Max from Deltalight) acts on the dark wall as accent lighting.
All the custom-made work was realised in oak and MDF, and varnished in a graphite colour.
The table (260x100 cm) of lacquered oak is Frederic Kielemoes' own design.

94-97
The hanging wall cupboard conceals the flat screen with sound installation and the bar cupboard.
The continuous, indirect lighting at the bottom of the cupboard emphasises the suspended effect.
Reading light Chantecaille from Christian Liaigre.

A hand basin in Buxy gris with a work surface and rear wall in brushed oak lacquered graphite.
Recessed T5-lighting on the work surface and ceiling lighting of the Carre type from Deltalight.

Frederic Kielemoes

Interior architect

Brugstraat 53

B – 8850 Ardooie

T +32 (0)486 40 75 64

www.frederickielemoes.be

info@frederickielemoes.be

CALMING AND FUNCTIONAL

Interior architect Filip Vanryckeghem (iXtra) ensured the total design of this new construction project, in a rural setting.

The attention was primarily paid to the ground floor, where the spatial layout was central, as was the connection between living room, stairwell, kitchen and dining room,...

The hearth wall offers a lockable storage area, e.g. for the flat screen and sound installation.

In the entrance hall the stairwell, cloakroom and toilet come together harmoniously.
The zenithal incidence of daylight (via the skylight at the top) ensures for transparency and a shadow play.
In the evening the Kreon fittings replace this function: a Side in-line uplighter on the wall and downlighters (Mini Side in-line) on the stairs.

Hand basin mirror with integrated LED-strip lighting.

The open living kitchen, with extendible dining table via an invisible sliding section, offers space for a maximum of ten persons.
Integrated base lighting in the wall and ceiling and specific Kreon construction fittings that ensure for a few light accents above the washing up and dining zone. Light profile: Kreon / Prologe 80 on-regule.

The bedroom, with two symmetrically set-up, sliding dressing room walls. This room connects directly to the entrance hall and the bathroom but can be closed off by the sliding partition.
Integrated ceiling spotlights from Kreon (Down in-Line 76).

The bathroom is behind the bedroom and forms a single whole. The suspended mirror cupboard with storage function and as a partition between the bath and shower zone includes an integrated TL-fitting at the bottom that fulfils the safety conditions (IP44 for wet rooms).
TL-lighting of the Lumco type, with separate ballast.

Shower, bath and hand basin were assembled ingeniously by Filip Vanryckeghem into a harmonious and functional whole. Various types of lights ensure a varied atmosphere: a TL-mirror cupboard, shower spotlights from Kreon (Down in-Line 76 with glass sealing (IP44-standard). The Small Diapason wall spots with shadow cap are also from Kreon.

[**iXtra**

Interior architecture

Filip Vanryckeghem

Ieperstraat 18

B – 8930 Menen

T +32 (0)474 31 19 74

www.ixtra.be

info@ixtra.be

[MONUMENTAL AND INTIMATE

Interior architect Filip Vanryckeghen transformed an existing, rather monumental extension into a full, pleasant living space.

In consultation with the customers the decision was taken to create a restrained, intimate atmosphere. The large space was consequently also divided, however without losing the larger cohesion.

The consistent general use of materials for each space contributed to the coherence and conviviality of this home environment.

The existing hearth was retained: it formed the start of the pattern in this interior.

The zenithal overhead light (via the skylight – is a thankful supplement to the lateral side light via the high window partition.

The additional artificial light (Diapason cover from Kreon) is integrated in the acoustic suspended ceiling via a type of light duct.

iXtra

Interior architecture
Filip Vanryckeghem
Ieperstraat 18
B – 8930 Menen
T +32 (0)474 31 19 74
www.ixtra.be
info@ixtra.be

BATHING IN LIGHT

T his bathroom set, created by the interior architect Filip Vanryckeghem (iXtra) forms a part of a renovation project in a bungalow designed by the architect A. Deheyter.

The elementary functions of the space (hand basin, bath, shower, sauna) were filled well but simultane-
ously an extra dimension was also striven for: a project that exudes "wellness".

The skylight above the 140x200 cm large bath from Kos provides extra
atmosphere both during the day and in the evening. The texture of the
coarse walls in natural stone creates additional play with light and shade.
In addition to the zenithal light there is also positive lateral daylight,
consciously obtained by opening the closed side façade over the entire
width and height of the bathroom.
Contact with nature outside gives a special dimension.

In the bathroom niche, integrated at the top: Kreon fittings, Side in-Line. The same type of Kreon Down in-Line 76 was opted for as general lighting (with glass in the shower in relation to the IP44-standard).

In the sauna room: a coloured TL-strip.

[**iXtra**

Interior architecture
Filip Vanryckeghem
Ieperstraat 18
B – 8930 Menen
T +32 (0)474 31 19 74
www.ixtra.be
info@ixtra.be

LIVING AND WORKING
IN PERFECT HARMONY

A rchitect Lie Ulenaers faced an important challenge when designing her own home and work space. She had to combine a very compact private residence with an office on the first floor.

The total design, furnishing and detailing result in an optimal division of both zones, which are still perfectly in harmony in a timeless atmosphere.

The consistently thorough white/black highlights reinforce the spatial effect. White gives continuous nuances according to the incidence of the light. As a neutral background this colour also constantly contrasts with the people and objects in the interior.
The limited materials and choice of colours ensure calm and coherence in all living spaces. The home was constructed in perfect consultation by the company Vincent Bruggen.

119-121
The painting is a custom work by Ruth Berger. The built-in spotlights are from Kreon, Down model. A carpet by Limited Edition.

The wooden fireplace is custom-made and realised with smooth lines between aged ceiling-height oak cupboards. A TV is also integrated here.
The oak coffee table is a unique creation realised by the Heerenhuis.
The lighting in the living room is by Kreon: type Prologue 145.

Oak flooring with custom-made cloakroom cupboards in the entrance hall.
Kreon lighting, type Prologue 145.

An oak work surface on the white, custom-made cupboards was chosen for the laundry room. The door handles were made by a smith and are combined throughout the home with diverse cupboards. The lighting is by Luceplan Costanza.

A painting by Elisabeth Uytterhoeven hangs in the dining room. The calming green is the only highlight colour used in the kitchen and dining area.
The lighting is by Eden Design Sphere. The Oregon beam ceiling was whitewashed.

White Carrara marble was chosen as a kitchen floor. The white/black highlights on the work surface reinforce the whole in this living kitchen. The lighting is by Modular (Nomad) in a black finish. The kitchen was fully custom designed and furnished by Lie Ulenaers, as were all the built-in cupboards and custom-made parts of this home.

Oak parquet flooring was combined with a completely black/white interior in the office section. The reception table is by Netherlands design Spectrum Lino and is lit by Modular, Nomad type. The Maui chairs are from Kartell. The lighting above the work area is by Kreon (Regard Double type). Kreon lighting is used throughout the home so that some calm is given out by the colours, lighting and materials.

The bathroom is furnished without a bath but with a large walk-in shower. Built-in cupboards are located behind the mirrors above the hand basins.

Beside lights by Philippe Starck Miss K.

130
You can reach the dressing room from the bathroom. The dressing rooms were custom designed by Lieke Ulenaers and realised by Vincent Bruggen. The sober black/white line is consistently continued here.

[**Lie Ulenaers Architects**

   Molenstraat 70

   B – 3960 Bree

   T +32 (0)89 46 50 09

   M +32 (0)495 59 52 45

   www.architectulenaers.be

   info@architectulenaers.be

in partnership with:

Vincent Bruggen Villabouw

   www.vincentbruggen.be

The children's rooms are located on the third floor. Standing lights by Luceplan (Costanza).

The hall and living room are separated by a solid oak door.

LIGHT DEFINES THE ATMOSPHERE: PROJECT R25

A nversa Residential Housing is specialized in the design and total coordination of renovation, restoration and new construction projects: special realizations for special people.

This report shows their recently finished project "R25" in Brasschaat.

Anversa designed both the architecture and the interior of this home.

The light study was provided by Kurve.

The lighting is functional and sometimes theatrical.
Light defines the atmosphere everywhere in this home: not the fitting but the light *itself* is exceptionally important.
The objects are thereby given all necessary attention.
The small artwork against the wall in the hall is from Art & Language.
The stairs were lime-washed.

The home is experienced by some visitors as though they are in an art gallery. The owners' dream is to be able to add more art to the home in due course.
The whole is extremely light, calming and exudes a holiday feel.
The walls and even the cupboards are washed in snow white. The contrasting people and objects are the main focal point.

Pure lines. Bright architecture. Genuine and natural materials from here.
The parquet floor is nevertheless reminiscent of the pitched façades in New York.
The weathered character was the starting point.
On the right there is an atmospheric light from Mario Fortuny.

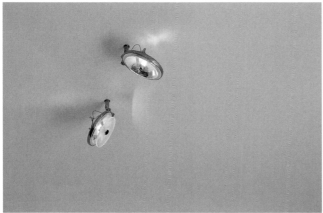

The Mexcal-spots from the Home Lighting collection by Kurve.

The photograph of Sugimoto is lit by two Mexcal-spots.

The table and chairs in the dining room are a design by Eero Saarinen.
The other furniture was custom-made.

The fittings from Volevatch ensure a timeless touch to the kitchen. A stove from La Cornue.

Y chair dining chairs by Hans J. Wegner around the dining table and a prototype wooden recliner by Verner Panton in the corner of the room.

On the first storey all the floors were
whitewashed, a finish by Dankers.

[**Anversa**

Divisie van KG73 bvba

Reintjesbeek 25

B – 2930 Brasschaat

T +32 (0)3 292 58 58

F +32 (0)3 292 57 57

M +32 (0)495 65 50 50

www.anversa.be

kg@anversa.be

[**Kurve Lichttechniek Waasland bvba**

Light consultants and lighting

wholesaler

www.kurve.be

AN INNOVATIVE STYLE

With a wink to the traffic ZONEdertig (the interior design office of Tiene Laurent and Frank Tahon) wants to slow down, consider, respectfully approach the living environment of its customers.

ZONE means the space in which the existence, life, movement of the individual takes precedence.

ZONEdertig stands for pure, timeless, honest, secure, no nonsense architecture, in which sincere design with harmonious colouring takes precedence.
Their projects testify to expertise, organisational functionality and a passion for beauty and detail.

Feng Shui, an over 3000 year old philosophy that teaches how the environment can influence happiness, is a foundation pillar. ZONEdertig has developed a special, innovative style that has grown from a symbiosis of two attuned opposites, an asset in the creation of both private and commercial projects.

The ceiling of this living space is lit in general with dimming built-in spotlights, Carree by Deltalight, which are switched in different circuits.
The organic form of the light over the table, Muse from Axolight, contrasts through its spicy form and harmonises in colour and atmosphere.

The blue partition is always accentuated in the four wind
directions by an LED fitting, Look In by Deltalight.
Combined with the colour this composition gives an
extremely soft and yet irresistible look in the evening.

⌈ **ZONEdertig interior architects**
⌊   Dudzeelsesteenweg 66
     B - 8000 Bruges
     T +32 (0)499 4145 81
     www.zonedertig.be
     info@zonedertig.be

The indirect T5, Speedline, takes you in the
direction of the corridor and allows the
atmospheric bath zone, equipped with Orbit Fix
built-in spots, to come fully into its own.

A LUXURIOUS AND REFINED RETREAT

This project is the result of the good cooperation between the owners (passionate art collectors) and interior architect Guillaume Da Silva, who took on the complete restoration of this well situated Brussels Town house (450 m² iving area).

The aim was to expose the original architecture and to restore it authentically.

The small rooms were preserved in this and transformed into intimate, pleasant living spaces.

This interior, designed as a curiosity cabinet, stages the objects and artworks of the owners thanks to an ingenious play on perspectives, materials and a sophisticated play on light. Striving for refinements in this way ensures a harmonious and comfortable, luxurious feeling that fits completely in the lifestyle and expectations of the owners.

The entrance hall with its majestic stairs is the true backbone of this home that extends over three storeys. "Medusa" chandeliers from Baxter, wall paper by Arte.

The original tiling and wood panelling in the entrance hall were restored in detail.

The dining room is an intimate space that comes into its full splendour in the evening, in the candlelight of dinners where refinement and conviviality go hand in hand.

As in every realisation by Guillaume Da Silva the kitchen is also of primordial importance here: a place where meals are prepared but also a place for exchanges and tasting.
The central La Cornue cooking island structures the room and provides axes.
The custom-made parts, designed by Guillaume Da Silva, are clad in glossy red lacquer.
A painting by Chantal Maskens.
The kitchen work surface and the floor were covered in natural stone from Vinalmont.

The living room on the first floor with a fireplace covered with mother of pearl like a jewel. The stucco plaster ceilings and parquet floor were fully restored.

The library is an intimate place, literally a curiosity cabinet where there is lots of space to store the many books and objects.

The bathroom of the lady of the house is undoubtedly the most glamorous room in this town house. Bisazza mosaic, Foscarini lighting and furniture designed by Guillaume Da Silva.

[**Guillaume Da Silva**

Interior architect

C.F.A.I

12, rue du Bois

F- 59100 ROUBAIX

T : + 33 3 20 11 12 62

www.guillaumedasilva.com

gdasilva@nornet.fr

Decoration: Mahogany (Doornik).

170
The master bathroom is a masculine room. A single material (black glass mosaic from Bisazza) for the floors, walls and the furniture creates power and simplicity in this room.

[SOUL AND FEELING

This rehabilitation takes p ace in a recently built house of 550 m². The new owner did not identify with the existing spaces and wanted to have a living space that fitted better with their image, so appealed to interior architect Guillaume Da Silva to give "soul and feeling" again to this too conventional architecture.

View from the kitchen to the living room:
creation of perspectives and superposition of
foregrounds and backgrounds. Posts structure
and define the spaces wh le keeping them open.

The living room axis is provided by the stained brushed and grooved oak chimneybreast.
Low table and lamps from Baxter. Sofa from Ascension Latore.

The hall: a rough oak parquet floor with a patina from ammonia and a wall covered in wallpaper from Elitis.

The WC is a too often neglected room; Guillaume Da Silva created a space with a genuine concept.

The kitchen plays an extremely important role.
The island realised in black granite structures the room and gives it its axes that define the preparation area and the dining area.
The cupboards make it possible to conceal all the technical elements.

The small dining room for intimate meals by candlelight.
Wallpaper form Arte and a suspended light from Ascension Latore.

The entrance situated between the barn section and the new build allows the distribution of the spaces.
This room sets the general tone and the resolutely off-beat style of the house for the visitor.
Painted brick walls, zinc patina doors and black varnished joinery.

In the bathroom, the bath tub leaning against American walnut panelling creates the separation to the dressing room. The cladding of the bath is realised in Vinalmont stone. The monumental shower was realised in tadelakt by Odilon Créations, with a Vinalmont stone floor.

The bedroom is decorated with wallpaper from Arte. Beside lights by Jaime Hayon.

The dressing room was designed as a semi-open room on the bathroom and in direct connection to the bedroom. All the fixtures were designed by Guillaume Da Silva and custom made in American walnut.

The reception room.

Situated in an old 150 m² barn adjoining the house, this room is entirely dedicated to the owner's friends.

As this space is more particularly intended for the evening and night, Guillaume Da Silva created a place where the juxtapositions and contrasts of the materials give life to scenic lighting: contrast and cohabitation of rough and more sophisticated materials.

Equipped like a disco, it allows the organisation of receptions that are both prestigious and convivial.

The 5 m long chimneybreast is realised in rough sheets and black granite, the floors are in black concrete. On the wall gold leaf panelling are combined with black painted brick.

"Joséphine" light from Metal Arte designed by Jaime Hayon. Furniture by Baxter.

[**Guillaume Da Silva**

Interior architect

C.F.A.I

12, rue du Bois

F- 59100 ROUBAIX

T : + 33 3 20 11 12 62

www.guillaumedasilva.com

gdasilva@nornet.fr

Décoration Mahogany (Tournai)

DARING MISE EN SCÈNE

In this old arms factory transformed into a loft on two floors, the architect Henri Simonis and the interior architect Eric Franssens made a strong statement and installed a perspective which, from entry, is uncovered on a concrete wall, followed by the steel band of the staircase.

The glazing integrated in the roof allows zenithal light to enter, bathing the ground floor that is essentially made up of the living room, kitchen and a new independent area where the cloakroom and utility room are located. In perfect combination, the lighting emphasises the coarse structure of the concrete thanks to suspended ceilings, unhooked and provided with light gorges, and highlights the architecture, giving strength to the space. The home automation offers the possibility of modulating the intensity of the light for unique and always varying atmospheres.

This very soft lighting that imitates the natural light may be compensated by four light tubes from the Iride light by Pierre Luigi Nicolin for Artemide. B&O speakers.

Under the double glazing with oak strips (Entreprises Demarche de Barchon) which illuminates until the ground floor, arranged through hanging lamps of Castore by Artemide of different diameters.

To light this spectacular bison, Trimless triples from Modular are integrated in the ceiling linking the Metamorphosi Yang Touch by Artemide placed on the ground in front of the black planilaque cube (Saint-Gobain) which holds the cloakrooms and utility room.

The concrete canvas serves as a wall for an L-shaped office the furniture of which was custom designed by Eric Franssens. In coloured MDF, it is accompanied by chairs by Verner Panton and has a light Globo di Luce by Roberto Menghi for Fontana Arte on top and at the back Bulb by Ingo Maurer.

The structures of the cross pieces are emphasised by the fluorescent Speed Line tubes from Ed-Dis with LTB cover, connected on the kitchen side, to Donuts by Modular.

In the living room, the essentially vintage furniture from the great names and prestigious Italian design brands: B&B for the sofas. Eileen Grey (Classicon) for the occasional tables, Zanotta for the low tables, Le Corbusier and Eames (Vitra) for the chaises longues. At the back on the right, a Taccia light by the brothers Castiglioni for Flos and, on the left, Pipistrello de Gae Aulenti for Martinelli Luce. B&O speakers and screens. Trimless spots by Modular.

The kitchen (Leicht) varnished white with black polished granite work surfaces only allows a single tinge of colour, that from the Campari Light suspended lights by Ingo Maurer. Along the wall, behind the counter, five modules form a six metre long piece of furniture, without handles. The central block has two Novy hoods above it that cover the cooking segment and are embellished with Bombo stools by Magis. Plumbing fittings by Dornbracht. The tall elements (refrigerator, oven, wine cellar) are grouped together a little to the side. The Tulip de Saarinen table and chairs for Knoll are lit by Arco lighting by the brothers Castiglioni for Flos. The Donuts ceiling lights and Trimless spots equipped with AR111 lights from Modular provide an agreeable lighting.

In the cloakroom, the Half Pipe suspensions by Modular lead to the Corian block with Vola plumbing fittings, designed by Eric Franssens. It is surrounded by a back-lit mirror with Speed Line from Ed-Dis fluorescent tubes. The two doors to the right give out to separate toilets equipped with a double Slide by Modular. Starck sanitary facilities for Duravit.

Henri Simonis Architecture

Rue des Vennes 324

B – 4020 Liège

T +32 (0)43 44 22 03

F +32 (0)43 44 22 02

M +32 (0)475 22 88 48

www.henrisimonis.be

simonishenri@skynet.be

Eric Franssens

Interior architecte

Rue des Bruyères 133

B – 4000 Liège (Cointe)

T +32 (0)4 25 40 999

F +32 (0)4 25 40 998

M +32 (0)475 32 99 15

www.ericfranssens.com

The bathroom with black glass paste mosaics (Bisazza) has a Spazio bath tub by Kos placed on a metal arch while the floor surface shower uses Clear-Shield glazing (Saint-Gobain) which limits the stains and allows the easy flow of water. Viega basin and plumbing fittings Axor de Starck for Hansgrohe. Intro spot by Modular with a 50 W dichroic bulb. The LED Strip by Niko emphases the cavity wall.

[ADDRESSES]

Anversa
Divisie van KG73 bvba
Reintjesbeek 25
B – 2930 Brasschaat
T +32 (0)3 292 58 58
F +32 (0)3 292 57 57
M +32 (0)495 65 50 50
www.anversa.be
kg@anversa.be
P. 132-151

Brick in the Wall NV
E. Bekaertlaan 53
B - 8790 Waregem
T +32 (0)56 60 40 90
F +32 (0)56 60 87 26
www.brickinthewall.eu
P. 25, 37, 55, 65

Guillaume Da Silva
Interior architect
C.F.A.I
12, rue du Bois
F- 59100 ROUBAIX
T : + 33 3 20 11 12 62
www.guillaumedasilva.com
gdasilva@nornet.fr
Decoration: Mahogany (Doornik).
P. 156-185

Deltalight Belux
Muizelstraat 2
B - 8560 Wevelgem
T +32 (0)56 435 735
F +32 (0)56 435 736
www.deltalight.com
P. 20, 35, 49-51, 55, 69, 76-79

Hugo-Neumann NV
Industriepark 5 zone A
B - 1440 Wauthier-Braine
www.hugo-neumann.com
P. 36, 83

iXtra
Interior architecture
Filip Vanryckeghem
Ieperstraat 18
B – 8930 Menen
T +32 (0)474 31 19 74
www.ixtra.be
info@ixtra.be
P. 100-115

Eric Franssens
Interior architect
Rue des Bruyères 133
B – 4000 Liège (Cointe)
T +32 (0)4 25 40 999
F +32 (0)4 25 40 998
M +32 (0)475 32 99 15
www.ericfranssens.com
P. 186-195

Frederic Kielemoes
Interior architect
Brugstraat 53
B – 8850 Ardooie
T +32 (0)486 40 75 64
www.frederickielemoes.be
info@frederickielemoes.be
P. 86-99

Kreon

Industrieweg Noord 1152

B - 3660 Opglabbeek

T +32 (0)89 51 96 22

F +32 (0)89 51 96 20

www.kreon.com

P. 16-19, 28-31, 40-42, 44-47,

52, 54, 56-64, 70-74

Kurve Lichttechniek Waasland bvba

Light consultants and lighting wholesaler

www.kurve.be

P. 132-151

Modular Lighting Instruments

Armoedestraat 71

B - 8800 Roeselare

T +32 (0)51 26 56 56

www.supermodular.com

P. 21, 32, 33, 38-39, 68, 82

PVD Verlichting BVBA

Kapelsesteenweg 597

B - 2180 Ekeren

T +32 (0)3 605 34 00

F +32 (0)3 605 39 17

www.pvdverlichting.be

P. 24, 66-67, 80-81

Henri Simonis Architecture

Rue des Vennes 324

B – 4020 Liège

T +32 (0)43 44 22 03

F +32 (0)43 44 22 02

M +32 (0)475 22 88 48

www.henrisimonis.be

simonshenri@skynet.be

P. 186-195

Lie Ulenaers Architects

Molerstraat 70

B – 3960 Bree

T +32 (0)89 46 50 09

M +32 (0)495 59 52 45

www.architectulenaers.be

info@architectulenaers.be

in partnership with:

Vincent Bruggen Villabouw

www.vincentbruggen.be

P. 116-131

Wever & Ducré

Beversesteenweg 565

B - 8800 Roeselare

T +32 (0)51 23 24 40

www.wever-ducre.com

P. 22-23, 34, 43, 48, 53, 55, 65, 75

ZONEdertig interior architects

Dudzeelsesteenweg 66

B - 8000 Bruges

T +32 (0)499 4145 81

www.zonedertig.be

info@zonedertig.be

P. 152-155

PUBLISHER
BETA-PLUS Publishing
Termuninck 3
B - 7850 Edingen
www.betaplus.com
info@betaplus.com

PHOTOGRAPHY
All pictures: Jo Pauwels, except:
P. 16-19, 28-31, 40-42, 44-47, 52, 54, 56-64, 70-74: Kreon / Serge Brison
P. 20, 35, 49-51, 55, 69, 76-79: Deltalight
P. 21, 32, 33 onder, 68: Matthijs Van Roon
P. 22-23, 34, 43, 48, 53, 55, 65, 75: Wever & Ducré
P. 24, 66-67, 80-81: Arne Jennard
P. 25, 37, 55, 65: Brick in the Wall
P. 33 boven, 38-39, 82: Filip Dujardin
P. 36, 83: Clearlight / Kaslov Studios
P. 152-153: ZONEdertig
P. 186-195: Serge Brison

GRAPHIC DESIGN
POLYDEM
Nathalie Binart

TRANSLATION
Txt-Ibis

April 2010
ISBN 13: 978-90-8944-068-6